'10

D0229712

Wonderful Water

GO Green

Helen Lanz

W
FRANKLIN WATTS
LONDON•SYDNEY

First published in 2010 by
Franklin Watts
338 Euston Road
London NW1 3BH

Franklin Watts Australia
Level 17/207 Kent Street
Sydney NSW 2000

Series editor: Julia Bird
Design: D.R. ink
Art director: Jonathan Hair
Artworks: Mike Phillips

A CIP catalogue record for this book is available
from the British Library.

ISBN 978 0 7496 9271 1

Dewey classification: 333.9'1

Picture credits: G M B Akash/Panos: 15b;
Georgios Alexandris/istockphoto: 17;
Mikhail Bistrov/istockphoto: 27; Cristiano Burmester/Alamy: 13b;
Caro/Alamy: 11; Anthony Cooper/Ecoscene: 22; T Costin/
istockphoto: 21t;Claudia Dewald/istockphoto: 6b;
Chad Ehlers/Alamy: 13t; EPA: 19t;The Garden PL/Alamy: 23b;
Bill Grove/istockphoto: 25b;Chris Hepburn/istockphoto:
18l; Hippo The Water Saver ®: 21b;Ian Hubball/istockphoto: front cover
b; Image Source Pink/Alamy: 6t; Bonnie Jacobs/istockphoto: 23t;
Selina Joiner/istockphoto: 20;Thammarat Kaosombat/istockphoto: 10;
Ethan Myerson/istockphoto: 18r;Picture Partners/Alamy: 26t;
Giacomo Pirozzi/Panos: front cover t;Ragnarock/Shutterstock: 9t;
Recycle Now Partners: 26b; Ravi Tahilramani/istockphoto:15t;
Bridgit Taylor/DV/Getty Images: 16t; D Timiraos/istockphoto: 12;
Tishi/Shutterstock: 9b; Ken Welsh/Alamy: 25t;
Peng Wu/istockphoto: 24; Tania Zbrodko/Shutterstock: 16b;
Andrejs Zemdeya/istockphoto: 7.

To my mum because you're the stars in the sky and so on.

Every attempt has been made to clear copyright.
Should there be any inadvertent omission,
please apply to the publisher for rectification.

Printed in China

Franklin Watts is a division of Hachette Children's Books,
an Hachette UK company.
www.hachette.co.uk

"During 25 years of writing about the environment for the Guardian, I quickly realised that education was the first step to protecting the planet on which we all depend for survival. While the warning signs are everywhere that the earth is heating up and the climate changing, many of us have been too preoccupied with living our lives to notice what is going on in our wider environment. It seems to me that it is children who need to know what is happening: they are often more observant of what is going on around them. We need to help them to grow up respecting and preserving the natural world on which their future depends. By teaching them about the importance of water, energy and other key areas of life, we can be sure they will soon be influencing their parents' lifestyles, too. This is a series of books every child should read."

Paul Brown
Former environment correspondent
for the Guardian, environmental author
and fellow of Wolfson
College Cambridge

Contents

Words in **bold** can be found in the glossary on page 28.

Water for life

What have you done today? Have you had a drink, or cleaned your teeth? Maybe you've been for a bike ride? Many of the things you've done today will have used water in some way, from turning the tap on to get a drink, to making the bike you're riding.

Drink to survive

The most important use of water is for drinking. We cannot survive without drinking water. Children should drink between six and eight glasses of water every day. This helps your body to work properly, keeps you healthy and helps you to concentrate. Plants and animals rely on fresh water for life, too.

Did you know?
Elephants can smell water from a distance of around five kilometres.

 Drinking plenty of water helps to keep us healthy and alert. You should drink more water when you've been exercising.

 Like people and animals, all plants need water to survive.

An important ingredient

We don't just need water to drink, cook or wash in, we need it to make nearly everything we use, too. Water is needed to grow the foods we eat and to grow natural **materials**, such as cotton, used to make many of our clothes. It is also used in many of the processes to make things from drinks cans to the bricks we use to build our homes.

IT'S ALL ABOUT WATER

- **At birth, water makes up approximately 80% of a baby's body weight.**

- **Our skin is 70% water; our brain is 75% water.**

- **80% of the contents of a pineapple and 95% of the contents of a tomato are water.**

95%

What goes around

Did you know there is the same amount of water in the world today as when the Earth was formed over 4,500 million years ago? There are about 1,260 million trillion litres of water on our planet and it is always on the move. This is because of the **water cycle**.

The water cycle

2. These drops of water form clouds.

3. The water droplets in the clouds collect together and get bigger and heavier and fall as rain, sleet or snow.

1. Water in rivers, lakes and seas is heated by the Sun and turns into **water vapour**, or drops of water in the air.

4. The rain falls to the ground and runs back into rivers, lakes and seas, and the cycle begins all over again.

Did you know?

We drink the same water now as the dinosaurs did over 200 million years ago. That means that you have shared a drink with the dinosaurs!

Cheers!

A watery world

Seventy per cent of the Earth's surface is covered in water. But 97% of this is in the seas and oceans, so it is too salty for us to drink.

This picture of the Earth from space shows the blue seas and oceans.

GO GREEN!

Distribution of the world's water:

97% seawater

2% **ice caps** and **glaciers**

1% freshwater

Water is used for growing food all around the world.

Freshwater

Freshwater makes up just one per cent of the Earth's water. People depend on it for drinking, washing in, for **industry** or the processes used to make things, **agriculture** and many other uses.

Where our water goes

Although our water goes around in a loop, there are many more demands made on it today than in the past. We are using up our freshwater supplies more quickly than the water cycle can refill them.

What water is used for:

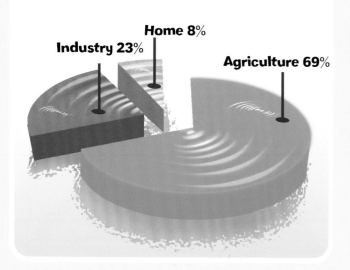

Home 8%

Industry 23%

Agriculture 69%

Food and water

Growing food uses by far the largest amount of our freshwater. The world's **population** has exploded in the last 100 years, growing from 1.2 billion people in 1900 to over six billion by 2000. That's a lot of mouths to feed!

Rice is usually grown in paddy fields. Rice needs a lot of water to make it grow, so the fields are often flooded by farmers.

Did you know?

Growing just one kilogram of rice uses up about 1,432 litres of water. That's the same as 18 full baths!

WATER USAGE AROUND THE WORLD

- Despite the fact that Australia's rainfall is the lowest of all the continents in the world (except Antarctica), Australians use more water per person than anywhere else in the world.

- Producing the food eaten by the average American each year takes 5.6 million litres of water – that's over two and a half Olympic-sized swimming pools of water per person!

Fashion and industry

The world's growing population uses more and more things, from clothes and toys to homes and transport. Industry uses up the next largest amount of water after agriculture. It takes 8,000 litres of water – that's enough to fill 100 baths – to make just one pair of leather shoes, for example.

Water in the home

At home we use water for drinking, washing, cooking and so on. In **developed countries** (the UK, Australia and the USA, for example), our water is cleaned before and after we use it. This is expensive and uses a lot of **energy**.

 Water is used in almost all industries, including the metal-working industry, where it is used for cooling.

Water footprint

Have you ever thought about your **water footprint**? No – not the footprint you leave on the bathmat – the amount of water you use!

Direct and indirect

Here's how a water footprint works. We use water in two ways: direct, or actual use, such as when we turn on the tap or flush the loo, and indirect use. This is the hidden amount of water that we don't use ourselves, but that has been used to make or grow what we use or eat.

Down the drain

On average, every person in the developed world uses about 150 litres of direct water a day to eat, drink and wash in (that's nearly two full baths); but nearly 30 times as much again in indirect water. That's the same as flushing the loo more than 774 times in one day!

 Imagine filling your bath over 50 times in one day. That's about the same amount as your water footprint.

Someone else's water

Our water footprint may not only be large, it may also cover a huge distance. Often things we eat, drink or use in this country have been made a long way away, using up water which may be in short supply in someone else's country.

These people in Zimbabwe, Africa, are tending to rows of crops. The crops will be sold all over the world.

CASE STUDY

MAKING A CAN OF FIZZY DRINK

 Sugar cane is used to make sugar. Growing and processing it uses up lots of water.

A can of fizzy drink may contain only 0.35 litres of water, but it uses about 200 litres of water to grow the sugar that's in the drink and another 305 litres to make the can. The fizzy drink is the direct amount, the water used to grow the sugar and make the can is the indirect amount.

A changing climate

How we choose to live affects our **environment**. If we use a lot of water at home, travel a lot in cars or planes, or buy lots of new things, it doesn't just cost us money, it costs the environment, too.

The cost of living

We rely on burning the **fossil fuels** – coal, oil and gas – to produce energy in order to make things, grow things, keep our homes light and warm, or cook our food. The world's growing population is using more and more energy and this is having an impact on the world's climate.

2. The Earth has a layer of protective gases around it called the atmosphere. It allows the Sun's rays in, but also keeps in some of the Sun's heat. As more fuel is used, more greenhouse gases are added to the atmosphere. They are good at trapping heat, so more heat is kept in, warming the Earth up.

3. Rising temperatures have started to change the weather patterns around the world. This is called **climate change**.

1. Coal, oil and gas develop underground over millions of years. When they are burned, they create energy. Burning these fuels gives off a gas called carbon dioxide which is a **greenhouse gas**.

Warming up

The Earth's climate varies naturally, but people have made it change more quickly by burning more and more fossil fuels. We can already see the effects of climate change – some areas have hardly any rain, whilst others have too much. It is predicted that as more greenhouse gases go into the air the Earth's climate will warm up further, and some countries will become even drier. If this happens, our water will become even more precious.

⬆ ➡

As our climate changes, where it was once possible to grow food or live safely is changing too due to **drought** (above) and floods (right).

Did you know?

Four out of every ten people in the world are not able to get to clean water easily.

Cut down in the kitchen

The good news is that it is easy to save water every day. And what's even better is that if we all do it we can make even bigger savings.

Chill!

Did you know that every time you run the tap waiting for the water to run cold to get a cold drink, you waste about nine litres of water a minute? That is nearly a whole bucket of water down the drain. Instead of doing that, just fill up a jug with water and put it in the fridge.

It takes a lot of water and energy to make a can.

Water kept in the fridge is cold and refreshing.

A healthy choice

Next time you are thirsty, instead of reaching for a can or bottle of drink, just have a glass of water. Not only is this much more healthy than drinking fizzy drinks or cordials, it is much better for the environment, too, because you're not using a can or bottle. Remember, it takes water to make these as well as fill them.

TAP FACTS

- **On average, a family in the USA will turn the tap on between 70–100 times a day.**
- **In Britain in the 1830s, each person used about 18 litres of water a day; by 1930 this had risen to 126 litres. Today, it is about 150 litres a day.**

Two for the price of one!

If you are boiling vegetables, try to just cover them with water – any more is a waste!

Who does the cooking in your house? Remind them to use only the amount of water needed when it comes to cooking vegetables or boiling the kettle. This not only saves on water, but also on the energy needed to make the water boil.

Lighten the load

There is more good news! We can save water at home when we do the washing-up and laundry, too.

Doing the dishes

Many homes now have a dishwasher. So which is best – washing by hand or using a dishwasher? A dishwasher uses about 15 litres of water compared to a washing-up bowl, which holds about six litres. But if you wash up by hand a few times during the day, you can use more water than in the dishwasher.

 Research has shown that washing the dishes by hand doesn't always save water.

As long as you scrape, but don't rinse, the plates first, and wait until the dishwasher is full before turning it on, studies have shown that using the right dishwasher saves both water and energy.

SAVING ENERGY

If you need a new appliance, such as a dishwasher or washing machine, talk to your mum or dad about choosing one that is energy-efficient. Look at the labels – such as the Energy Star, European Energy label or the Energy Saving Recommended labels. These show which appliances use less water and energy, and so will be better for the environment.

Clean clothes

Each time you turn on the washing machine, it uses about 95 litres of water (that's about 380 glasses!) so only put your clothes in to be washed when they need it. And like the dishwasher, turn the washing machine on only when it is full.

Did you know?

Using an energy-efficient washing machine can save more water in one year than one person drinks in their whole lifetime!

Bathroom basics

There are lots of things you can do to save water in the bathroom – and still get clean!

Turn off the tap

Do you leave the tap running when you clean your teeth? That sends nine litres of water down the drain every minute. If you clean your teeth for three minutes (like you should!) that's 27 litres of water wasted each time you clean your teeth. Save that over a week, and you'll have enough water to splash around in a paddling pool.

Turn the tap off every time you brush your teeth. It will save enough water to splash in the pool on a sunny day!

HOW MUCH?

 Taking a bath uses around 80 litres of water.

 Taking a shower uses five litres of water per minute. A power shower can use up to ten litres of water a minute.

 Flushing the toilet uses up to nine litres of water – over half a bucketful.

Don't soak!

Filling a bath can use much more water than taking a shower, unless you have a power shower. If you have a five-minute shower instead of a bath, you can save about 55 litres of water. That's enough water to make about 220 cups of tea!

Only some showers save water. A power shower can use up to three times more water than having a bath.

CASE STUDY

FEELING FLUSH

Did you know that we probably flush away as much water in a day as we drink in a whole month? Old-fashioned single-flush toilets use up to about nine litres of water a flush; modern dual-flush toilets use up to six litres. If you have an old-fashioned toilet, contact your local water company to see if they supply water-saving devices such as a Water Hippo™. Or just fill up an empty drinks bottle with water and put that in your cistern.

The Water Hippo™ fits in the toilet cistern, taking up space so that less water is needed for each flush.

Waiting for a rainy day

A lot of water wasted in the home is actually wasted outside – in the garden or washing the car.

Storing water

Have you got a **water butt** outside? This can collect up to 5,000 litres of rainwater a year – enough water to fill 10 medium-sized paddling pools. You can use this to water both indoor and outdoor plants when the weather is dry.

Remember to put a lid on your water butt. This keeps the water clean and stops leaves falling into it.

Did you know?

A garden sprinkler left to water the grass for an hour can use as much water as a family of four does in one day.

Hide the hose

If you help to wash the car, be sure to do it with a bucket and sponge, rather than a hose. Hoses can use up to 1,000 litres of water an hour – that's enough to fill 12.5 baths full of water. You can save water by using water from your water butt rather than the tap.

Thank you very mulch!

Have you ever heard of mulch? It's a mixture of wet grass or bark and leaves. If you have a garden or allotment, it can be put around your plants to help the soil stay damp. It means you don't have to water your garden as often, and so is another good way to save water.

↑ Washing the car with a bucket and sponge can save a lot of water.

↓ A layer of mulch helps to keep soil moist.

Down the drain!

It is a good idea to look around your home for drips and leaks – mending these can save lots of water.

⬆ Remember to turn the tap off completely when you have finished using it.

Drip, drip

A dripping tap can waste more than 90 litres of water a week – that's more than a bath full. If you find a tap or pipe is leaking, tell your mum or dad so that they can fix it themselves or call in a plumber.

Every little helps

Save used washing-up water from the kitchen by collecting it in a jug or watering can. Rather than pouring it down the sink, use it to water any house plants or flowers in the garden.

Did you know?
A dripping tap can waste up to a bucketful of water a day.

Careful cleaning

Be careful about what goes down the drain. Any fluids you wash away join the water system, so put down as few **chemicals** as possible. If you help with the shopping, look out for cleaning products that are eco-friendly – these are designed to be kinder to the environment.

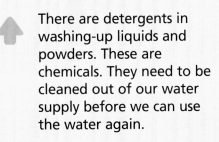
There are detergents in washing-up liquids and powders. These are chemicals. They need to be cleaned out of our water supply before we can use the water again.

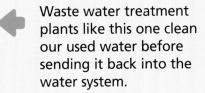
Waste water treatment plants like this one clean our used water before sending it back into the water system.

LEAKY FACTS

- **If every household in the USA had a tap that leaked one drop every second, 3,500 million litres of water would leak away each day. That is the same as 1,687 Olympic-sized swimming pools full of wasted water every day!**

- **By mending a dripping tap, you could save up to 5,500 litres of water a year – nearly 69 full baths.**

Pass on a glass!

Have you heard of the three Rs – reduce, reuse, recycle? That is just what we need to do with our water.

Step-by-step

First, we need to reduce how much water we use to help save it in the first place. We can reuse it in our homes and gardens to water plants rather than let it run down the drain. When possible, we can buy things made from **recycled** materials – this often uses much less water than making something from scratch.

 Use old washing-up water to water the plants in your garden.

CASE STUDY

RECYCLED PAPER

It saves at least 30,000 litres of water – that is a milk tanker's worth – to make one tonne of recycled paper, rather than making paper from new materials. It also saves enough energy to run a three-bedroom house for one year and reduces the amount of air pollution by 95%. That has got to be a win-win situation!

You can help to recycle paper by making sure that there are no staples or plastics mixed in with the paper you are recycling.

 Water is a precious resource that helps to make our Earth as beautiful as it is.

Cheers!

Cheers!

Small changes, big difference

Make small changes to how you use water every day. Remember, even a small change, if we all make it, will make a big difference. We need to make good choices so we can preserve our water and ensure that your children can share a drink with a dinosaur too!

Glossary

Agriculture Farming.

Chemicals Something that has been made through a chemical process. For example, detergents are chemicals that clean by removing dirt particles.

Climate change Longterm changes to the Earth's weather patterns.

Developed countries Countries that are wealthy and rely on money from industry; and where most people work in factories and businesses rather than agriculture.

Drought Where there is a shortage of rain over a long period of time.

Dual-flush A toilet that has two buttons so you can flush with a full cistern of water or part-cistern, to save water.

Energy This is the power needed to make or do something. Electricity is a form of energy.

Environment Surroundings.

Fossil fuels Fuels such as coal, oil or gas, which have developed under the ground from rotting animal and plant life over millions of years.

Glaciers A very slow moving mass of ice that has formed over many years by layers of snow building up on top of each other and hardening.

Greenhouse gas Carbon dioxide and methane are greenhouse gases. They create an invisible layer around the Earth, trapping in the heat of the Sun's rays.

Ice caps A layer of ice and snow that covers a large area of land all year round.

Industry Factories and businesses that make things.

Materials What something is made from, such as cotton, wood or metal.

Population The number of people living in a place.

Recycle To process a product so that the materials that it is made from can be used again.

Water butt A container to catch and store rainwater.

Water cycle The way our water supply moves throughout our environment.

Water footprint The amount of water a person, company or country uses per day. It is made up of direct water use – the water we drink, cook with or wash with - and indirect water use – the water that has been used to make the things we buy or use.

Water vapour Tiny water droplets in the air that form together to make clouds.

Useful information

Throughout this book, 'real life measurements' are used for reference. These measurements are not exact, but give a sense of just how much an amount of water is, or what it looks like.

 1 cup or glass full 0.25 LITRES

 1 bucketful 14 LITRES

 1 full bath 80 LITRES

 1 average-sized paddling pool 495 LITRES

 **1 milk tanker 30,000 LITRES**

 Olympic-sized swimming pool 2,500,000 LITRES

Further reading

Earth Watch: Water for All by Sally Morgan (Franklin Watts, 2005)

Green Team: Using Water by Sally Hewitt (Franklin Watts, 2008)

Exploring Earth's Resources by Sharon Katz Cooper (Heinemann, 2007)

Websites

www.captainsplosh.co.uk
A bright, informative website about where water comes from and how we should look after it.

www.thewaterschool.co.uk
A fun, interactive website with lots of tips on saving water.

www.wateraid.org
A worldwide charity that aims to bring clean water to everyone.

Dates to remember

World Water Day – 22 March
Set up by the United Nations in 1993, it is a day to think about how we use water and our global water resources. Visit www.worldwaterday.org.

World Food Day – 16 October
Set up by the Food and Agriculture Organization (FAO), part of the United Nations, in 1979 to draw attention to world food shortages. Visit www.fao.org.

Note to parents and teachers: Every effort has been made by the Publishers to ensure that these websites are suitable for children, that they are of the highest educational value, and that they contain no inappropriate or offensive material. However, because of the nature of the Internet, it is impossible to guarantee that the contents of these sites will not be altered. We strongly advise that Internet access is supervised by a responsible adult.

Index